Growing Up in
Mexico

Other titles in the *Growing Up Around the World* series include:

Growing Up in Brazil

Growing Up in Canada

Growing Up in China

Growing Up in Germany

Growing Up in India

Growing Up in Iran

Growing Up in Italy

Growing Up in Japan

Growing Up in Russia

Growing Up in
Mexico

Barbara Sheen

San Diego, CA

© 2018 ReferencePoint Press, Inc.
Printed in the United States

For more information, contact:
ReferencePoint Press, Inc.
PO Box 27779
San Diego, CA 92198
www.ReferencePointPress.com

LIBRARY OF CONGRESS CATALOGING-IN-PUBLICATION DATA

Name: Sheen, Barbara, author.
Title: Growing Up in Mexico/by Barbara Sheen.
Description: San Diego, CA: ReferencePoint Press, [2018] | Series: Growing
  Up Around the world | Audience: Grade 9 to 12. | Includes bibliographical
  references and index.
Identifiers: LCCN 2016056807 (print) | LCCN 2017019603 (ebook) | ISBN
  9781682822227 (eBook) | ISBN 9781682822210 (hardback)
Subjects: LCSH: Children—Mexico—Juvenile literature. |
  Youth—Mexico—Juvenile literature. | Mexico—Social life and
  customs—Juvenile literature.
Classification: LCC HQ792.M48 (ebook) | LCC HQ792.M48 S54 2018 (print) | DDC
  305.230972--dc23
LC record available at https://lccn.loc.gov/2016056807

CONTENTS

Mexico at a Glance	6
Chapter One A Nation of Contrasts	8
Chapter Two Family: The Heart of Mexico	19
Chapter Three School and Work	31
Chapter Four Social Life	43
Chapter Five Religious Influences	55
Source Notes	67
For Further Research	71
Index	73
Picture Credits	79
About the Author	80

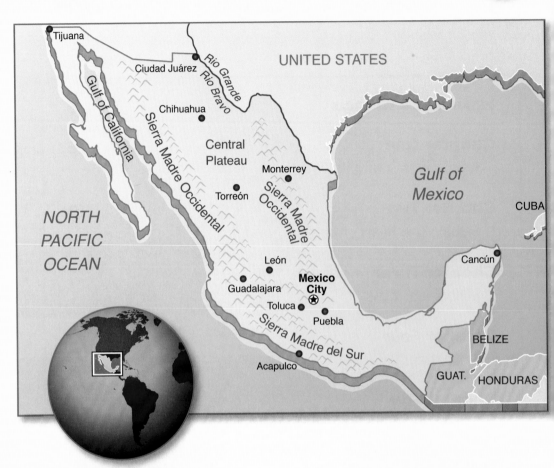

Tijuana

Ciudad Juárez

Río Grande
Río Bravo

UNITED STATES

Chihuahua

Gulf of California

Sierra Madre Occidental

Central Plateau

Monterrey

Sierra Madre Occidental

Torreón

NORTH PACIFIC OCEAN

Gulf of Mexico

CUBA

León

Cancún

Guadalajara

Mexico City ✪

Toluca

Puebla

Sierra Madre del Sur

Acapulco

BELIZE

GUAT.

HONDURAS

Official Name
United Mexican States

Capital •
Mexico City

Size
758,449 square miles
(1,964,375 sq. km)

Total Population
123,166,749 as of 2016

Currency •
Mexican peso

Youth Population
0–14 years: 27.26%
15–24 years: 17.72%

Religion
Roman Catholic: 82.7%
Pentecostal: 1.6%; Jehovah's
Witnesses: 1.4%; other Evangelical
churches: 5%; other 1.9%

Type of Government
Federal presidential republic

Language
Spanish (92.7%), plus 62
indigenous languages

Literacy •
95.1% (age 15+ able to
read and write)

Industries
Food and beverages, tobacco,
chemicals, iron and steel, petroleum,
mining, textiles, clothing, motor
vehicles, consumer durables, tourism

Internet Users •
69.915 million, or 57.4% of population

CHAPTER ONE

A Nation of Contrasts

When people think of Mexico, they often picture sugary white beaches, vibrant colors, spicy foods, and huge fiestas. These certainly are a part of Mexico, but there is much more to this diverse nation. Mexico is a land of contrasts. Here, artisans use skills that have been passed down for generations to create one-of-a-kind handicrafts, while large factories mass-produce cars, computers, and other items vital to twenty-first-century life. It is a nation where sixteenth-century churches and towering skyscrapers sit on ancient ruins.

Within its borders are huge cities where snarled traffic, noise, crime, and air pollution are the norm. Not far from this chaos, farmers tend fields of corn, and donkeys carry loads of kindling along dusty rural roads. It is a country in which great wealth and overwhelming poverty coexist, where the children of the wealthy attend private schools and wear designer clothes, while those who are much less fortunate beg on the street. The commonalities and contrasts that characterize this nation influence the lives of its youth. Young people growing up in Mexico share a rich cultural heritage. Yet depending on where they live and their economic status, their lifestyles can be quite different.

Diverse Geography

When it comes to Mexico's geography, diversity is the key. Covering 758,449 square miles (1,964,375 sq. km), Mexico is the fifth-largest country in the Western Hemisphere. It borders the United States in the north (abutting California, Arizona, New Mexico, and Texas); Guatemala and Belize in the south; the Gulf of Mexico in the east; and the Pacific Ocean in the west. Within its borders are rugged mountains, deep canyons, steamy rain forests, and vast deserts. It contains 5,797 miles (9,330 km) of coastline and more than three thousand volcanoes. Its two largest mountain ranges surround the nation's heartland. This area, which is known as the central plateau, contains Mexico's most fertile soil and three of its major cities—Mexico City, Guadalajara, and Puebla. And it is where most young Mexicans live.

Mexico's climate is also diverse. Regions located in the central plateau have a temperate climate. Areas in the high mountains get snow. Low-lying areas have a tropical climate, while desert regions are arid. The variations in climate and terrain make Mexico one of the world's most biologically diverse nations on earth. In fact, 10 percent of all known animal species on earth and about twenty-six thousand species of plants can be found in Mexico. Corn, tropical fruit, wheat, beans, chile peppers, and cotton are among the many crops cultivated by Mexican farmers. Mexico is also rich in natural resources like silver and is the world's sixth-largest producer of oil.

Young people growing up in such a diverse nation have different experiences depending on where they live. For instance, young people living on the coasts may swim, fish, and surf for fun. Some work in resort hotels that cater to vacationers. Teens growing up in northern Mexico often live on ranches, where they ride horses and raise animals. Young people from southern regions are likely to be Amerindian. Many speak ancient indigenous languages and have limited contact with people of other cultures. Those living in cities bordering the United States have a much different experience. Most make frequent trips across the border to neighboring cities, where they are exposed firsthand to American life and culture. As Arena, a young woman who grew up along the Mexico-Texas border, explains:

> Growing up in Juarez was very different than in any other place in Mexico, we are very accustomed to the "American way of life", so we are a mix of Mexican values and American customs. . . . For many a typical Saturday would be to . . . cross the border . . . go shopping at the mall in El Paso [Texas], eat some Chinese food, then go to Wal-Mart buy your groceries and come back to Juarez.[1]

The Ek Balam Mayan architectural site rises from the lowlands of Mexico's Yucatan Peninsula. The fifth largest country in the Western Hemisphere, Mexico contains diverse geographical regions, including this one.

A Rich History and Culture

No matter where young Mexicans grow up, Mexico's history and culture bind them together. Historians think that Mexico has been inhabited for about fifteen thousand years. It was the home of a number of advanced ancient indigenous civilizations, including the Mayan and Aztecan. These civilizations built large cities and tall pyramids. They had writing systems, structured societies, and advanced knowledge of mathematics and astronomy. Today the ruins of these ancient civilizations dot Mexico's landscape and are a point of pride for many young Mexicans.

The last of Mexico's great indigenous civilizations—that of the Aztecs—was destroyed by the Spanish explorer Hernán Cortés and his men in 1521. Mexico soon became a Spanish colony. Among the new arrivals were Catholic priests, who converted the indigenous population. Spanish settlers built towns and cities resembling those in Spain, with churches and central plazas. Many of the male colonists took Amerindian mistresses. Their mixed-race offspring, known as mestizos, became the ancestors of most modern Mexicans. In fact, the nation observes a holiday known as the Day of Race celebrating this intermingling.

Mexico gained its independence from Spain in 1821; it then fell under French rule from 1862 to 1867. Poor conditions in the country led to a bloody revolution in 1910 that pitted rich against poor and laid the groundwork for modern Mexico.

Mexico's history shaped its national identity, which is a mixture of Spanish and indigenous cultures. Young people growing up in Mexico study its ancient cultures in school and visit archaeological sites. They live in cities and villages with central plazas and colonial churches. They observe holidays that celebrate Mexico's independence from Spain and France. Most identify as Catholics, although many combine native customs in their religious practices. And even though sixty-two indigenous languages are still spoken in Mexico, the majority of young Mexicans speak Spanish. Moreover, most Mexicans identify as mestizo, which to Mexican teens means that their culture incorporates elements from both Amerindian and Spanish traditions. Victor, a young Mexican artist, uses the term *mestizaje*—which means the mingling of the two races and cultures—as he explains: "Mexico is a fusion of two civilizations, the Spanish and the indigenous. We are both, half and half. It is mestizaje, the joining, and we are mere by-products of that merging."[2]

> "Mexico is a fusion of two civilizations, the Spanish and the indigenous. We are both, half and half. It is mestizaje, the joining, and we are mere by-products of that merging."[2]
>
> —Victor, a young Mexican artist

A Young and Growing Population

Indeed, approximately 60 percent of Mexico's population is mestizo. An estimated 30 percent are Amerindian, and 10 percent are of purely European or other ancestry. Together they constitute more than 123 million people, making Mexico the tenth most populous nation in the world. Mexico is also among the fastest-growing nations. According to the Pew Research Center, its population is predicted to grow by 32 percent by 2050.

Mexico is also one of the youngest countries in the world. Approximately half of all Mexicans are under age twenty. This has led

Violent Crime and the Drug Trade

Violent crime is a problem in Mexico. Much of it is tied to warring drug syndicates or cartels. The cartels smuggle illegal drugs from Mexico into the United States. Some of the drugs, like marijuana, and opium poppies, are grown in Mexico. Other drugs, like cocaine, are moved northward from other Latin American countries through Mexico to the United States by Mexican drug gangs. The cartels also produce and smuggle synthetic drugs, such as ecstasy and methamphetamine, which they sell in the United States. The smugglers have been known to illegally purchase assault weapons in the United States, which they use against their rivals in Mexico. However, it is not uncommon for innocent people to get caught in the violence.

Mexican drug cartels recruit adolescents to work for them. Most are young, poor males who have dropped out of school. In fact, more than 75 percent of minors arrested on drug charges in Mexico are young males. These young men are charged with smuggling the drugs across the border. Some are trained as assassins, whose job is to kill members of other cartels. Once these youngsters become members of a drug gang, they are not permitted to quit. Doing so is typically met with violence to the gang member and his loved ones. As of 2016 more than one hundred thousand Mexicans have been killed as a result of drug-related violence.

to problems. Schools are overcrowded. Classrooms crammed with fifty or more students are common. Many schools do not have enough desks, books, or teachers to go around and often run split shifts to accommodate the large number of students.

The size and youthfulness of Mexico's population also affects the job market. Every year more than 1 million young people enter Mexico's job market. There are not enough jobs for these job seekers, making competition for work intense and leading to high unemployment among Mexico's youth. In 2014, for example, Mexico's total unemployment rate was 4.8 percent, but that same year the unemployment rate for Mexicans ages fifteen to twenty-four was 9.6 percent.

In order to find a job, many of these young people flock to Mexico's largest cities, where overcrowding has worsened crime, traffic, and pollution and where the high cost of living adds to their struggle. Some become involved in illegal activities, such as drug trafficking or prostitution, in order to survive. Others hike for days, risking dehydration, heat stroke, and even death in search of work in the United States.

Modern Cities

Approximately 79 percent of all Mexicans reside in urban areas. There are nine cities in Mexico with a population of 1 million or more and sixteen cities with a population of at least five hundred thousand. The nation's capital and largest city, Mexico City, is the third most populous city in the world. The city itself is home to more than 12 million people, while an additional 8 million individuals live in Mexico City's metropolitan area. About one-third of the residents of Mexico City and its metropolitan area are between the ages of fifteen and twenty-one.

Young people growing up in Mexico's cities have access to many of the features that characterize urban life in the United States. Visiting libraries and museums and attending sporting events and concerts are a part of many wealthy and middle-class urban Mexican teens' lives. So is seeing newly released movies at the multiplex, hanging out with friends at shopping malls, and strolling through tree-lined parks and plazas. People often get to these places by using public transportation. Indeed, Mexico City's

Mexico's capital, Mexico City, is the third most populous city in the world. Around one third of the people who reside there or in the surrounding metropolitan area are between the ages of fifteen and twenty-one.

Metro underground rail system is the second largest in North America, carrying over 1 billion passengers per year.

In most Mexican cities street vendors are everywhere. They dart through traffic, tempting gridlocked drivers with savory snacks. They set up kiosks on street corners, where they sell everything from tacos to T-shirts. Some sit on the sidewalks with their wares spread on colorful woven blankets. Beggars and street performers are also part of the urban scene. Many are poor children, adolescents, and teens whose families depend on their earnings to survive.

Some are homeless and destitute. Known as street children, many of these youngsters were orphaned or abandoned. Approximately fifteen thousand street children under age eighteen live in Mexico City. These boys and girls sleep rough in doorways, sewers, and makeshift encampments in parks. They do whatever it takes to earn enough money to survive. For example, Gustavo, a homeless teenager, lies shirtless atop shards of glass in Metro stations begging for tips. As he explains: "Staying alive in this town means putting your body on the line . . . I've done everything from washing windscreens to selling my body to perverts."[3] Many of these youngsters sniff glue or other solvents as a way to briefly escape their problems. They are frequently the victims of violent crimes, as well as the perpetrators of illegal activities themselves.

For these unfortunate young people, growing up in Mexico's urban areas can be brutal. But life is not perfect for more privileged urban teens either. Teens growing up in Mexico's largest cities are exposed to high levels of air pollution, which can negatively affect their health. Indeed, it is not unusual for harmful chemicals trapped in the air in Mexico City to reach toxic levels. Mexico City resident Daniel Hernandez describes how this affects him: "I hack up alien-looking green phlegm in the mornings for weeks at a time."[4]

> "Staying alive in this town means putting your body on the line. . . . I've done everything from washing windscreens to selling my body to perverts."[3]
>
> —Gustavo, a Mexico City street child

Traditional Villages

Young people growing up in Mexico's rural villages live a more traditional lifestyle. In fact, in many cases their day-to-day life is not

Young Mexicans in rural areas often live in villages with simple dwellings. Many maintain a traditional agricultural lifestyle that is not much different from that of their ancestors.

very different from that of their ancestors. For instance, lots of rural teens do not have access to indoor plumbing. Many rural homes get their water from a pipe system located outside the home or from a public faucet. Although most rural homes have access to electricity and most families have a television, it is rare for young people growing up in these areas to have computers or Internet access. Some villages are too remote to have telephone lines or cell phone towers. Bloggers Jim and Mindy Phypers, an American couple who live in a small Mexican village, explain: "We keep in touch with the world and maintain our website with a satellite dish installed in the back yard. We are the only folks in town to be connected to the Internet or to own a computer. . . . Three of us in town have managed to pick up a cell phone signal from a nearby town using a high-gain antenna on a tall mast. No land lines were ever installed here."[5]

There are few economic opportunities in these villages, and most rural Mexicans subsist by cultivating small plots of land. For farmers, the workday extends from sunrise to sunset. Children and teens work beside their parents mending fences, cleaning pens, caring for livestock, and tending crops. Many drop out of school at a young age so they can work full time. When harvests are good, young rural Mexicans have plenty to eat. However, when harvests are poor, they may face periods of food insecurity.

Government

Whether Mexican teens grow up in a bustling city or a quiet rural community, every city, town, and village in Mexico is part of a state or federal district. Mexico is divided into thirty-one states and one federal district. The nation's official name is the United Mexican States. Each state and municipality has its own governing entities, but the ultimate authority is the federal government. As in all nations, governmental decisions impact the lives of all citizens—young and old.

Mexico is a democracy and a federal republic with three branches of government: legislative, judicial, and executive. The legislators and president are elected by popular vote, while Supreme Court justices are appointed by the president. Young Mexicans can legally vote at age eighteen. They are guaranteed the right to an education by the nation's constitution. Schools follow a national curriculum that is determined by the federal government. As a result, no matter which state young people reside in, their studies are basically the same.

Another part of the constitution that directly affects Mexico's young prohibits child labor. However, this regulation is commonly ignored. According to the World Bank, millions of minors work in Mexico. Approximately 870,000 of these young workers are under age thirteen.

Mexico's Indigenous People

Mexico's indigenous people are descendants of the people who lived in Mexico before the arrival of the Spanish. According to the Mexican national census, in 2015 more than 25 million people, many of whom are children and adolescents, identified as being indigenous. Most of Mexico's indigenous people live in the nation's southern states, which are also among Mexico's poorest states.

Indeed, many of Mexico's indigenous people live in extreme poverty. They often lack access to health care and have a higher infant mortality rate than the nonindigenous population. Some do not speak Spanish, which makes it difficult for them to succeed in school. Many drop out of school as children, and some never attend. These factors lessen their employability. Recently, many young indigenous Mexicans have organized and/or participated in protests and demonstrations to raise awareness of the inequalities indigenous people face. As a result, the government has instituted a number of social development programs aimed at helping indigenous people.

Many Challenges

Like all nations, Mexico has problems. Among the most significant is economic inequality. Although Mexico has the thirteenth largest economy in the world, approximately 46 percent of the population falls below the poverty level. Ten percent of these individuals live in extreme poverty. To put this in perspective, the Mexican government defines poverty as living on no more than 2,329 pesos ($123) per month in cities and 1,490 pesos ($79) in rural areas. It defines extreme poverty as living on no more than 1,125 pesos ($59) per month in cities and 800 pesos ($42) in rural areas. "Poor health, hunger, dirt floors, cardboard roofs, and a lack of electricity and plumbing are their inheritance," author and Mexican resident Carol M. Merchasin says of the extreme poor. "They sit on the streets and beg, make a few tortillas or pick wildflowers to sell."[6]

Among the impoverished are more than 24 million children and adolescents under age eighteen. Youngsters growing up in poverty typically experience worse material living conditions and a lower quality of life than their more privileged peers. Indeed, many poor Mexican children have limited access to health care. Some live in makeshift housing without running water or sewage, and many suffer from malnutrition, anemia, and stunted growth. In contrast, many of Mexico's middle class and wealthy children live in gated communities designed to keep the poor out. Indeed, Mexico's richest 1 percent owns 43 percent of Mexico's wealth.

The Mexican government is taking steps to improve income inequality. Through a program known as Prosper, mothers who live below the poverty level receive a cash stipend from the government under the conditions that they keep their children in school, take their children for regular visits to a health clinic, and attend monthly nutrition classes. The program is designed to keep young Mexicans well fed and healthy. As Sixta, a mother of six, explains: "The money we get . . . helps a lot. Right when we run out of money, money comes in, and we can buy the things we need to get by."[7] The program also makes it possible for children to stay in school, which should help them get good-paying jobs in the future.

Prosper appears to be helping. But it is not a complete solution to the problem of poverty. Many young Mexicans are demanding that the government do more. They have conducted demonstrations to bring attention to a number of issues facing their country, including economic inequalities.

Mexico's large youthful population is the nation's future. These youths are charged with doing what they can to move their country forward while still embracing the many commonalities and contrasts that define Mexico.

CHAPTER TWO

Family: The Heart of Mexico

The family is at the heart of Mexican society. Immediate and extended family members are dedicated to supporting each other. Large and small problems are shared, as are ordinary and extraordinary triumphs. Family members work together to fix stalled cars and leaky roofs, help each other find employment, and care for each other when they are sick. As Roberto, a Mexican man, explains: "We watch out for one another. That's what counts."[8]

From an early age, Mexican children are taught to put the needs of their family before their own needs. This is known as *familismo* (familism). Familismo is an essential part of Mexican life and culture. As Mexican resident Carol M. Merchasin explains: "The unconscious question for Mexicans is, 'What do I need to do to serve these people who are my support?' The not-so-unconscious question for Western cultures is, 'What is best for me?'"[9]

The Nuclear Family

Most Mexican children grow up in a traditional nuclear family consisting of a mother, father, and siblings. An estimated 74.2 percent of Mexican families fall into this category. The average age for couples to marry is twenty-three for women and twenty-six for men. And most Mexican youngsters have at least one sibling. On average, urban couples have two or three children, while rural couples have three to six.

Traditionally, Mexican families are patriarchal in structure. The father is typically the chief decision maker and the primary breadwinner. His authority is rarely challenged. Mexicans use the term *machismo* (assertive masculinity) to describe this traditional male role.

A mother's traditional family role is described by the term *marianismo* (submissive femininity). Even if she is among the 44 percent of Mexican women who work outside the home, she is responsible for the family's health and welfare. She runs the household and cares for the children. In Mexican culture the mother is considered the soul of the family, and she is usually revered by her children.

Children, in turn, are doted upon by their parents. At the same time, they are expected to be respectful of all family members. Rebelliousness is frowned upon. "Family comes first. Teenagers stay close to home and have a stronger commitment to their parents than many American teens do. . . . Families enforce dependence on each other,"[10] says family counselor Marcelina Hardy.

As a matter of fact, parents and children generally maintain extremely close ties even after the children are grown. Such ties are reflected in living arrangements. Unlike in the United States, most Mexican young adults do not move out of their family home until they get married. And many do not leave even after they wed. Instead, their spouse moves into the family home, too. This allows young couples to save up enough money to eventually set up their own household. It also makes it easy for grandmothers to help young mothers care for their children. Amy, a young American woman who lives with her husband Carlos's parents in Mexico, explains:

> "Family comes first. Teenagers stay close to home and have a stronger commitment to their parents than many American teens do."[10]
>
> —Marcelina Hardy, freelance writer and mental health counselor

Right now, all three of my mother-in-law's kids are living at home. That includes Carlos and I, his older sister and her husband, and Carlos' younger, [adult] unmarried sister. . . . It is not considered imposing if a son or daughter stays at home until he or she is married and even after. And when babies are born, children once again come home or mothers move in with their daughters to help with the baby. For example . . . last Christmas, Carlos' sister found out she was pregnant. They [the sister and her spouse] let the lease on their apartment run out and they moved back home. The problem was, where would they sleep. . . . The solution to the problem was to move the younger sister out of her bedroom so that the older sister and her husband could sleep in the bedroom with the new baby. The younger sister was moved to the couch in the TV room . . . sacrifices are willingly made to accommodate family.[11]

A Mexican woman brushes her young granddaughter's hair. Most Mexican children grow up amid an extended family that consists of both blood relatives and close family friends.

Extended Families

Most Mexican youngsters grow up with close ties to their extended families, which include blood relatives as well as close family friends. In fact, extended family members often live in the same house or neighborhood. "Close ties," author Roberto Campa-Mada explains, "are maintained through constant visits, mutual support, trips taken together, family reunions, and so on."[12] It is common for cousins to grow up together, almost like siblings. Their aunts and uncles treat them in much the same way as they do their own children, not hesitating to shower attention and praise on them or to discipline them, depending on the circumstances. No one feels that they are overextending their boundaries, because child rearing is frequently a group activity in Mexico. Older siblings are expected to look after younger brothers and sisters, and grandmothers often care for babies and toddlers while mothers work outside the home.

Godparents, too, are a vital part of extended families. Before a baby is baptized in Mexico, the infant's parents choose the child's godparents. Godparents do not have to be a married couple or even a relative. Anyone close to the family may be selected. Being a godparent is an honor, but it also comes with lifelong responsibilities. Godparents are charged with giving their godchild spiritual, emotional, and material support throughout the godchild's life. Even when they are adults, godchildren can turn to their godparents for advice and help in almost any matter. And if something should happen to the child's natural parents, godparents are there to help. For example, even though Juan Pablo is poor, when the father of his two godchildren was killed, Juan Pablo helped provide for the children. He explains: "I am the padrino [godfather] . . . so I must help them—money, food, school supplies, clothing, backpacks. It is a big responsibility."[13]

Some Mexican youngsters have more than one set of godparents. The godparents selected at a child's baptism are the most significant godparents in a young person's life. However, families often select additional "event godparents," whose role is largely financial. Event godparents help sponsor important rites of passage in a youngster's life. First Communion godparents, for instance, may buy the frilly white dress or little suit the child wears,

Family Names

In Mexico families are identified by a combination of both parents' family names. Most Mexican children's names consist of a first name, a middle name, and a double last name, which consists of the father's first surname (his father's family name) followed by the mother's first surname (her father's family name). For example, the name Juan Carlos Ramirez Garcia consists of a man's given name, Juan; his middle name, Carlos; his father's family name, Ramirez; and his mother's family name, Garcia. If Juan Carlos marries a woman named Elena Maria Baca Silva, his name does not change. Elena Maria's name, however, does. She keeps her father's family name, Baca, and drops her mother's family name, Silva. It is replaced by her husband's family name, Ramirez. Therefore, her new name is Elena Maria Baca Ramirez.

If Juan Carlos and Elena Maria have a child whom they name Diego Abel, the child's full name would be Diego Abel Ramirez Baca. And if the couple has a second son and names him after the father, that child's full name would be Juan Carlos Ramirez Baca, distinguishing his name from his father's, Juan Carlos Ramirez Garcia. Therefore, there is no need to add "Junior" to the son's name to distinguish his name from his father's.

while wedding godparents help pay for the wedding reception. Event godparents do not bear the same responsibilities as baptism godparents, but they provide children and teens additional trusted adults in their lives.

Mexican Homes

The homes Mexican families live in vary greatly, depending on the location and the family's income. Upper- and middle-income Mexican teens usually reside in comfortable houses and apartments. Homes in urban areas, where crime can be a problem, may be in high-rise apartment buildings that are protected day and night by security guards. Other urban and rural homes of this income group are likely to consist of brightly colored, sturdy, cement block houses situated behind high outside walls topped with spikes or broken glass. The walls shield the houses from the street and help prevent burglaries.

Many homes are built around a central exterior courtyard. It is here that caged birds chirp, families relax, and children play away from the street. Most of these houses have flat roofs that are accessed by an outdoor staircase. Families often have parties on the roofs, which may also house a satellite dish, a container garden, a clothesline where laundry is hung to dry, and a small tank where extra water is stored.

These homes are furnished in much the same way as American homes, and young people growing up in them enjoy many of the same amenities as their northern peers. Many have their own bedroom, while some share a room with a sibling. These youngsters typically have access to a computer or tablet, a CD player, and a cable or satellite TV system that broadcasts Mexican and American programs. Many people can access the Internet from their homes, and most have their own smartphones. Author Daniel Hernandez describes the home of Alfredo, a middle-class resident of Mexico City and a member of Hernandez's extended family: "At Don Alfredo's home, I meet his wife, Doña Sabina, and

Homes in Mexico's urban areas are often painted in bright, vibrant colors. Houses in the city of Guanajuato (pictured) provide one vivid example.

his son Alfredo, and Alfredo's wife Silvia and two small children, Carolina and Job. They have a comfortable and modest house, wedged between other houses with brightly painted exteriors. Inside I enter a warm space of tiled floors and wooden furniture. . . . Two bedrooms and a bath are upstairs, and a garden on the roof."[14] (*Don* and *Doña* are terms of respect sometimes used in Spanish.)

In contrast, poor families are often crammed into tiny houses that contain just one or two rooms—a common area and sometimes a bedroom. There may also be a small lean-to outdoors where mothers build a cooking fire with wood gathered by young family members. There is usually a latrine but no running water piped directly into the house. Sewage from the latrine is rarely treated, and it is common for streets and ravines to contain raw sewage.

These homes are likely to have dirt floors and corrugated metal roofs. The walls may be made of cinder block or, in the worst cases, of thick cardboard stuffed with rags. Insulation in the latter is poor, and there is usually no heating source, making these homes cold and drafty in the winter. Furnishings are sparse. Young people rarely have any personal space. In fact, it is common for two or more siblings to share a bed. Nor do they usually have access to the modern electronics that more privileged teens take for granted.

Mealtime

No matter what type of home young Mexicans reside in, delicious aromas wafting from the kitchen bring families together. Children and teens usually have a light breakfast before hurrying off to school. Sweet bread, fresh and warm from the bakery, or refried beans spread on a hot corn tortilla and washed down with a steamy cup of hot chocolate are popular morning meals. Indeed, corn, beans, and chile peppers are staples of the Mexican diet, and there is almost always a pot of beans simmering on the stove in Mexican homes.

By midmorning, most youngsters' stomachs are growling. Schools give students a short break to have a little bite. Many students bring a snack with them. This can be anything from a few cookies, to a bag of corn chips flavored with lime and chile powder, to leftovers from an earlier meal. Mothers frequently arrive at the school right before snack time to deliver a hot burrito wrapped in foil to their children.

Most schools let out at noon. Vendors wait outside the gates, tempting homeward-bound students with little treats. For a few pesos, youngsters can buy snacks like hot sweet potatoes; corn on the cob sprinkled with cheese, lime juice, and chile powder; or freshly squeezed juices. Once they arrive home, they have time to do homework or household chores before the afternoon meal. It is eaten between two and four in the afternoon and is the main meal of the day. Most businesses close their doors at this time, only to reopen later, so that employees can go home and eat with their families. In middle- and high-income homes, the afternoon meal frequently begins with an appetizer like guacamole, which is a dish of mashed avocados that family members scoop up with crispy fried pork rinds or corn chips. Next comes a soup dish, which is usually a clear broth, followed by the main dish. It might be chicken, fish, or meat served with rice, a salad, and a stack of fresh, hot corn tortillas. Poorer families might enjoy stew or beans with hot tortillas, accompanied by rice. In any case, no matter what is served, the afternoon meal is a time for families to get together, talk, laugh, and share news of the day.

> "All family members participate, including small children who help out at an early age with household or field chores."[15]
>
> —Roberto Campa-Mada, Mexican author and scholar

After such a large meal, most stomachs are full. So supper, which is eaten around eight o'clock, is more of a snack than a full meal. It may be a repeat of breakfast, a small sandwich, or if teens are out and about, tacos purchased from a street vendor.

Everyone Helps Out

In most households, it is the mother's job to cook the meals. Some higher-income families have a housekeeper who does the cooking and cleaning. And although adolescents and teens in these circumstances have fewer responsibilities than their less privileged peers, most Mexican youngsters are expected to help out. Unlike in the United States, where parents may pay their children for doing chores, Mexican children and teens are rarely com-

Access to Water

Many young people growing up in Mexico do not have the same access to clean water as teens in the United States. As of 2015, according to the *CIA World Factbook*, 96.1 percent of all Mexicans have access to improved drinking water. However, these statistics are tricky. Access to improved water is defined as not only water piped into a home, but also water piped into a yard or plot of land, as well as water from a public tap, which may be a distance from the residence. The job of fetching and carrying water from the tap often falls to youngsters. Moreover, there is not always enough water to go around. Consequently, young people must be very careful about how much they use, making activities like bathing on a daily basis extremely difficult.

Even in the homes of wealthy and middle-class families, water scarcity can be an issue. In many cities the municipal water supply is turned off for a portion of the day. And even when water is available, water pressure in most homes is low. To ensure that family members have sufficient water, most families pay to have extra water delivered by truck. This water is stored in large black tanks on roofs or underground.

In addition, water in Mexico is rarely purified. Toxins in the water can cause disease. As a result, Mexico is the world's largest consumer of bottled water.

pensated for their efforts. According to Campa-Mada, "All family members participate, including small children who help out at an early age with household or field chores."[15]

Gender and the family's socioeconomic status impact what is expected of youngsters. Generally, while girls are charged with helping their mothers—doing chores like cooking, cleaning, laundry, caring for younger siblings or aging relatives—males do not contribute to household chores. In fact, in some families sisters are responsible for washing and ironing their brother's clothing and making his bed. If the family lives in a rural area, girls may also be responsible for helping take care of the animals. As one young girl explains: "Usually when I arrive home from school, I eat lunch by 3:00 P.M., finish my homework, help my mom with the rest of the chores in the house (like washing and hanging clothes to dry, dishes, sweeping, feeding the animals or tending the sheep on our farm), and finally go to bed around 9:00 P.M."[16]

This is not to say that boys have no responsibilities. Some families run a makeshift car wash out of their garage or driveway.

This type of physical labor falls to the boys, as do tasks like walking younger siblings to school or helping male relatives fix things around the house. Still other chores are shared by both boys and girls. They help out in family-run businesses, waiting on customers and stocking shelves in little stores; serving diners and busing tables in family-owned eateries; or making handicrafts that older relatives sell, among other jobs. As Merchasin explains, "Many workers in family businesses are young family members and the jefe [boss] is often a father, uncle, or brother-in-law, a padrino or godfather."[17]

Many Mexican teens and adolescents also work part time at other jobs. The poorest do odd jobs like selling newspapers or gum on the street or bagging groceries in supermarkets for tips. The money they earn is used to help support their families. "I like to help my mom,"[18] explains Eleuteria, a teen who spends most weekends selling food at a Mexico City train station along with her three siblings.

> "Many workers in family businesses are young family members and the jefe [boss] is often a father, uncle, or brother-in-law, a padrino or godfather."[17]
>
> —Carol M. Merchasin, author and resident of San Miguel de Allende, Mexico

Family Fun

Family life in Mexico is not all work. Close-knit families have fun together. Teens usually spend Friday nights and Saturdays hanging out with friends. But they stay home on Sunday, the day that is traditionally reserved for family activities. Typically, multiple generations of extended family get together on Sunday to share the afternoon meal, which may be anything from a rooftop barbeque, to a big family lunch prepared by all the women, to a group outing at a local restaurant. The get-together usually does not end when everyone finishes the meal. Families frequently linger for hours, chatting and laughing. As Maria Jose Cespedes, a young Mexican blogger, explains:

> Restaurants are even selected in terms of how comfortable they are for this activity, and waiters know that if a big table arrives it will most probably stay for a long time. On

weekends, restaurants start filling up at 3:00 pm. . . . Nowhere in Mexico will you be asked to leave after lunch, and kitchens usually never close. You can ask for more food at any time between lunch and dinner. Sobremesas [staying at the table to visit after a meal] are a perfect way to enjoy the company of friends and family, to catch up and to pass the time.[19]

Taking a walk or a bike ride after leaving the table is another part of a typical Sunday. In small towns and villages, families can be found strolling around the central plaza. Here adults leisurely

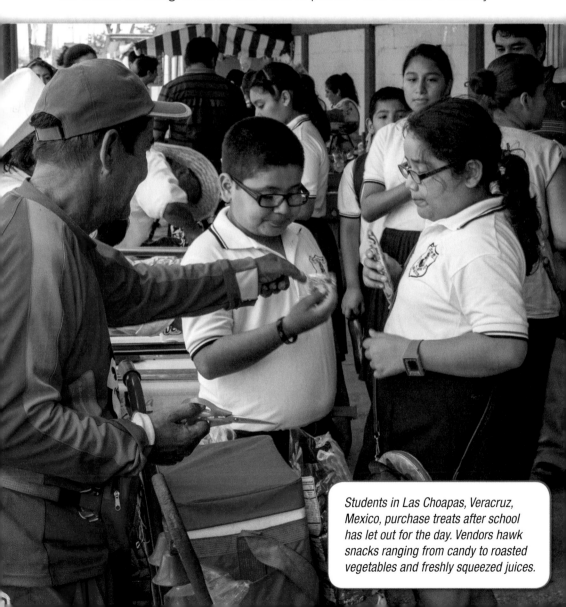

Students in Las Choapas, Veracruz, Mexico, purchase treats after school has let out for the day. Vendors hawk snacks ranging from candy to roasted vegetables and freshly squeezed juices.

amble about, elderly relatives sun themselves on wrought-iron benches, and teens and children visit with other local youngsters whose families are also enjoying a Sunday stroll. In big cities like Guadalajara and Mexico City, some major boulevards and avenues are closed to traffic so that families can stroll or bike safely. As Rommel Cesena, a young Mexican blogger, explains:

> If you ever find yourself in Guadalajara, Jalisco, Mexico on a Sunday afternoon, you might notice there are a lot of families about. Restaurants are full with them, parks are bustling with kids running around and even a few main arteries of the city are closed . . . transforming into the "Via Recreativa" (roughly translated as "the recreational avenue"), where families can cycle around and enjoy the city.[20]

Indeed, members of Mexican families like spending time with each other. For Mexican adolescents and teens, family comes first. Youngsters do whatever it takes to support their loved ones, who in turn do what they can to return this support.

CHAPTER THREE

School and Work

Getting an education is one of the best ways for young Mexicans to escape poverty. However, many youngsters leave school at age fourteen or younger to help support their families. Finding a good-paying job is not easy, especially for those with limited education.

Getting an Education

Education is compulsory for Mexicans ages three through fourteen. This translates to three years of preschool, followed by six years (grades one through six) of primary school, and three years of lower secondary school (grades seven through nine). Students are not required to continue their education beyond ninth grade, but about 56 percent go on to enroll in upper secondary or preparatory school (grades ten through twelve), which is the equivalent of high school.

Most students attend public schools. Public schools do not charge tuition. But students must purchase school supplies and school uniforms. Uniforms typically consist of a white shirt and grey slacks for boys and a pleated skirt and white blouse for girls. Despite laws requiring that children and teens attend school, some poor youngsters do not go to school because their families cannot afford these costs.

Those students who do attend public school face a number of challenges. Although the Mexican government has placed a strong emphasis on education as a way to reduce income inequality, because of insufficient funds and the sheer number of young Mexicans, many public schools are overcrowded. Most operate two sessions per day to accommodate all the students. The first shift usually begins at eight o'clock and runs until noon; the second begins around two o'clock and ends at six o'clock.

As preparatory school student Jonathan Fonseca Camarena explained, "I like the afternoon shift. Then I can hang with my friends at night, and do my homework in the morning before school."[21]

Overcrowding is not the only problem. Thousands of schools lack running water, indoor plumbing, electricity, heat, or cooling fans. Many have dirt floors and broken windows. Schools in coastal areas routinely flood during rainy season. In many instances there are not enough desks or chairs to go around. Youngsters are packed together on hard benches behind rickety desks that they have to share.

Schools in rural villages are frequently the most neglected. And it is difficult to attract qualified secondary-level teachers to isolated communities. To solve this problem about 3 million students in lower secondary school receive instruction via televised lessons. Each lesson takes about fifteen minutes. After each lesson, students have forty-five minutes to complete an assignment. An adult is on hand to provide assistance.

Rural students who want to go on to upper secondary school face other issues. There are few preparatory schools in rural areas. Many teens have to leave home to complete their education, an expense that most rural families cannot afford. Consequently, many rural teens leave school early.

Problems related to public schools lead some of the more privileged families to send their children to private schools that charge tuition. As of 2014, about 9 percent of Mexican teens attended private lower secondary schools, and about 18.6 percent attended private preparatory schools. Typically, these schools are in good condition, boasting on-campus media centers, science labs, athletic facilities, and the latest technology. To ensure that students become proficient in English, many employ both Spanish- and English-speaking teachers, and classes are often conducted in both languages.

These schools are prestigious. Standards are set high, paving the way for students to succeed in college and beyond. In fact, some private schools are affiliated with colleges that guarantee admission to affiliated graduates. Even without such a guarantee, more private school students go on to college than public school graduates. According to Roberto Campa-Mada, "These

Boys read textbooks in an Acapulco classroom. Although students are not required to complete education beyond ninth grade, about half of them do go on to enroll in schools teaching grades ten through twelve.

schools sell their image as shapers of future leaders. And, indeed, as flaunted in advertisements of these institutions, upon graduation alumni gain access to the best positions."[22]

Course Work, Exams, and Graduation

Mexico's schools follow a national curriculum, which is updated by the federal government every so often. Consequently, the course of study for both public and private school students are similar. Indeed, students in schools across Mexico have much in common. For instance, according to writer and editor H. James McLaughlin, "Every Monday there are patriotic exercises in which the children display the flag, sing the national anthem, and listen as adults exhort them to be respectful and conscientious students. Mid-morning there is a 'recreo' [recess], a break to eat snacks and play outside."[23]

The school year in Mexico runs from September through May. Primary and lower secondary students attend school five days per week. Preparatory students often attend classes on Satur-

Military Service

Young men in Mexico are required to sign up for the military at age eighteen. Once they sign up, their names are placed into a lottery system. Those whose names are chosen must perform one year of service. These young men are trained to protect Mexico's internal security in case of an uprising, counter drug-related operations, and help the civil population in case of a natural disaster. Most draftees train only on the weekends. Training includes physical fitness, as well as performing public service. Draftees rarely, if ever, fire a gun or receive marksmanship training. Most recruits come from poor families. For a fee, many young men from middle- and upper-income families get a physical deferment, which identifies them as physically unfit for service.

Draftees are not integrated into regular military units, which are made up of enlistees and military professionals. At age sixteen, young men who want more intense military training can enlist in Mexico's army, navy, or air force for an initial three-year term. Upon completion of this service, they are encouraged to reenlist and choose the military as their career. They can also attend military schools, which prepare them to serve as military officers upon graduation. Young women, too, can enlist in the military. However, their service is limited to medical and administrative activities.

day, too. In primary school, students study Spanish language arts, math, geography, history, art, and environmental science. When possible, indigenous students receive instruction in their native language, as well as being taught Spanish as a second language. According to McLaughlin, "Classroom life tends to be more informal than in U.S. schools. In many schools, students engage in frequent group work, often involving a great deal of student interaction and movement. At the same time, Mexican students are expected to show respect to the 'maestro/a' (the teacher)."[24]

The school day does not end for Mexican scholars when classes are dismissed. Mexican children and teens get lots of homework. Primary students get about one and a half hours of homework each night, while lower and upper secondary students are assigned up to three hours per night.

Students must pass an annual end-of-year exam to move from grade to grade. Some lower secondary schools also require that students successfully complete an entrance exam in order to enroll.

Lower secondary school is challenging. In addition to studying all the subjects covered in primary school, students take classes in English, geometry, algebra, and technology. The last may be hampered by a lack of computers. In these cases, teens practice keyboarding on sheets of paper printed to look like a computer keyboard. Class periods last fifty minutes and are followed by a ten-minute unsupervised break. Upon successfully completing lower secondary school, students are awarded a certificate. It, plus successful completion of a standardized exam, are required for admittance to preparatory school.

Teens entering preparatory school have to make some big decisions that their peers in the United States do not have to make. Studies on this level fall into two tracks: a vocational/technical track, which prepares students for lower-level technology and applied science careers; or an academic track, which prepares students for college. In much the same way as students pick a college major, preparatory students must pick a specialty field to concentrate on. Teens do not make this selection lightly, since this will also be their college major and future career field. As Laura Winfree, an American blogger who studied tourism administration in Mexico, explains: "My first semester of university in Cancun, many class conversations went way over my head because my Mexican classmates had been taking business-related courses since they were 15."[25]

> "Classroom life tends to be more informal than in U.S. schools. In many schools, students engage in frequent group work, often involving a great deal of student interaction and movement."[24]
>
> —H. James McLaughlin, writer, editor, and professor of education

Attending College

To gain admittance to college, teens must successfully complete another standardized test. Generally, students are ranked and admitted to college based on their test results and grade point average. Competition for admittance to public colleges is fierce, with more applicants than available places. As a result, upper secondary students spend a lot of time preparing for the test. It is common for wealthier students to hire private tutors to help them prepare for the exam.

Despite fierce competition for admittance, about 3.5 million Mexicans go on to college each year. Mexico has sixty-one public universities, with the largest enrolling over two hundred thousand students. There is also a large number of two-year technical and specialized schools and an estimated two thousand degree-granting private colleges.

Whether young people attend a private or public college, their experience is apt to be quite different from that of college students in the United States. For one thing, most Mexican colleges do not provide student housing. When possible, college students live at home with their families. If this is not feasible, they live with extended family members in distant cities. Or they rent a room in a stranger's home located near the college.

Another difference is that course work in Mexican colleges is often more demanding than in the United States, and an emphasis is placed on developing practical skills through internships and fieldwork. Getting hands-on experience is important because students can become licensed dentists, lawyers, and veterinarians, among other careers, by completing a five-year undergraduate program, or licensed physicians in six years. As Winfree explains: "I graduated from university here in Cancun 3 years ago. I studied Tourism Administration, a 4-year degree that required about twice as many courses as a U.S.A. university and no less than 5 internships, along with 240 hours of community service."[26] Moreover, many Mexican students hold down multiple jobs while attending college, making earning a degree even more challenging.

Finding Work

Mexico has a growing middle class. Many of these individuals work at jobs that require technical skills. In fact, Mexico is experiencing growth in high-tech industries like information technology and engineering, which means more job opportunities for young people with an education. According to a National Public Radio report by Mónica Ortiz Uribe, between 2003 and 2013, Mexico's high-tech industries grew three times faster than the world aver-

A young man fries food in a restaurant kitchen. About one fourth of Mexican youth ages twelve to eighteen work to earn money to help support their families.

age. A number of foreign-owned consumer electronics, software, banking, and biotechnology companies have opened offices in Mexico; these companies employ local managers, engineers, and information technologists. There is also an expanding number of Mexican-owned and operated high-tech businesses that have need for these professionals. For example, a number of Mexican software support companies provide assistance to businesses throughout the world. And software development start-up companies are popping up in many Mexican cities. Moreover, young educated Mexicans are needed to fill positions in health care, education, government, and more.

These types of jobs require completion of upper secondary school at a minimum. Although more young Mexicans are achieving this goal, almost half of the population leaves school by age fourteen to work. Approximately 25 percent of all twelve- to eighteen-year-olds in Mexico work. Most of these young people are poor. They work in order to help their families. Twelve-year-old Alejandrina Castillo is one of these children. She dropped out of school to work in the fields harvesting crops alongside her parents and siblings. "I work," she says, "because we need money to eat."[27]

Alejandrina's job pays very little. In a nation where more than 1 million adolescents and teens enter the job market each year, finding a good job is not easy for those with limited education. Since there are more employment opportunities in cities than in rural villages, many young people leave home to find work. Most of these job seekers have never been far from home before, and they miss their families desperately. As Carol M. Merchasin explains: "Leaving the family is an abandonment that goes against what Mexicans value most: the relationships that sustain them when all else fails. It is hard and painful."[28]

> "I work because we need money to eat."[27]
>
> —Alejandrina Castillo, Mexican child laborer

These youngsters are thrust into a situation in which they have to find a place to live, secure a job, and adjust to life in a strange place. Few own cars, and the cost of bus fare prevents them from going home to visit often. Eighteen-year-old Neftali Fuentes is one such teen. He left his family in southern Mexico to look for work along the US-Mexico border. "I was thinking the whole time about what I could do to send money back to my parents and how they were depending on that,"[29] Fuentes said.

Working Long Hours for Low Pay

For uneducated teens, finding a good-paying job is extremely difficult. Many wind up working in a maquiladora (a foreign-owned factory located in Mexico). Maquiladoras manufacture or assemble products for export. There are an estimated three thousand maquiladoras in Mexico, employing about 1 million Mexican workers, many of whom are young people.

Most maquiladoras are located in cities, where the cost of living is high. Many young maquiladora workers earn barely enough money to support themselves, making it practically impossible for them to send money home to their families. As of 2016, the minimum wage in Mexico was about fifty-eight cents per hour. Salaries for maquiladora workers range from minimum wage to about two dollars per hour for the most experienced workers. That translates to about $75 to $120 a week. Says

Young Female Maquiladora Workers Face Sexual Discrimination

Many maquiladora workers are young women. Young Mexican women can legally be hired to work in a maquiladora at age sixteen. However, many of these young workers get false documents in order to go to work when they are younger. It is not uncommon for girls as young as twelve to be employed by maquiladoras. Because young females are commonly paid less than their male counterparts in Mexico, maquiladora owners like to hire them. Moreover, according to a report by economist Mitali Shah, posted on Mt. Holyoke College's website, these young female laborers are commonly subjected to sexual discrimination.

For instance, in order to avoid hiring pregnant women, maquiladora owners may force prospective female workers to submit to a mandatory urine test to see if they are pregnant. Prospective female workers may be questioned about their sexual habits and their use of contraceptives. Already employed young women may also be required to submit to pregnancy tests. If they are pregnant, they may be forced to work unpaid overtime or be reassigned to more physically challenging work in an effort to make them resign. This protects the employer from having to provide the young workers with maternity benefits. Although the Mexican government forbids sexual discrimination, this law is often ignored.

Hugo Franco, a maquiladora manager, "Labor's cheaper here. You can pay people all day for what would be less than an hour's work in the states."[30]

Working conditions in many maquiladoras are poor. Plants often lack adequate ventilation, and young workers are expected to work up to ten hours per day, six days a week. Compensation and working conditions in other jobs that require little education—such as a construction worker, maid or server in a resort hotel, or crop harvester—are often worse. Nor are these jobs easy to come by.

For this reason, an estimated half of all Mexican workers turn to the informal or underground economy to earn a living. Some young workers in the informal economy do odd jobs or work in private homes as domestic servants. Most work as street vendors. Many set up carts and kiosks on streets, while others zigzag through busy traffic hawking anything and everything. A number ride bicycles carrying pots of hot foods that they peddle. Juan has been selling tamales in this way since he was fifteen. "I ride the bike every day from miles away on the other side of the city," he said. "I go to the city center and then I peddle here. I work all day and part of the night. I get up at 6 a.m., I get home at midnight."[31]

Working in the informal economy is tough. Street vendors work in all types of weather, seven days a week. At best, earnings are minimal. Such positions lack job security or a contract that spells out working conditions, hours, and wages. As economist David Lozano explains, "In many cases families turn to the informal economy so as to subsist."[32]

For many workers in the informal economy, missing a day's work means that they cannot afford to eat. And daily earnings are inconsistent. Leonardo, a young man who works in the informal economy, explains, "On a good day, I can make up to 600 pesos (about $35) but another day I might only make 50 pesos ($3)."[33]

Crossing the Border

Low pay and lack of employment opportunities cause many young Mexicans to try to illegally cross the border into the United States in search of better jobs. "I want to go to the U.S. because here [in Mexico] money doesn't stretch out," said Mary Lou Hidalgo, a twenty-one-year-old maquiladora worker and mother of two children. "People can't work in minimum-wage jobs at a maquiladora and educate themselves. If I want to be anything more or want better for my children, I have to find another way."[34]

> "Most Mexicans don't want to leave Mexico. They would much rather stay where the culture, language and values are familiar and their own."[35]
>
> —Laureno, an undocumented Mexican worker currently living in the United States

Getting safely across the border is risky. Northern Mexico's desert terrain is rough and desolate. Deaths due to heat and dehydration occur. And the US Border Patrol is on alert day and night. Individuals who are captured are sent back to Mexico. As a result, many young Mexicans endure multiple attempts in an effort to successfully get across.

A US Border Patrol agent takes a teen boy trying to enter the United States illegally into custody. Low pay and the lack of employment or educational opportunities in their home country prompt many Mexicans to attempt the journey north in search of a better life.

Once in the United States, undocumented immigrants risk being deported at any time. Since these individuals are in the country illegally, their employment opportunities are limited. Still, most earn more than they could in Mexico and are able to send money home to their families. However, being far from family and friends and constantly under the threat of deportation makes life for these undocumented young people very difficult. Some manage to save up enough money that they can go back to Mexico and start a small business. But for many, doing so is only a dream. As Laureno, a young undocumented worker, explains, "Most Mexicans don't want to leave Mexico. They would much rather stay where the culture, language and values are familiar and their own. But the economic and working structure in Mexico doesn't give them a chance to stay."[35]

Indeed, it is difficult for poor Mexican teens to earn a decent living in Mexico. Completing their education is the best way for these youngsters to join Mexico's growing middle class. With at least an upper secondary certificate in hand, these young people should be able to gain the type of employment that will help them prosper.

CHAPTER FOUR

Social Life

Mexican adolescents and teens like to have fun. Many of the things they enjoy doing are similar to what young people like to do throughout the world. Other activities are distinctively Mexican. Economic factors influence how young people spend their free time and what they do for entertainment.

Friendships

Hanging out with friends is a fun activity that almost all adolescents and teens enjoy. Affluent youngsters like to get together to play video games and watch movies, DVDs, and YouTube videos. In urban areas, they cruise shopping malls where they buy things, eat at food courts, and see newly released national and international movies. The latter either have subtitles or are dubbed in Spanish. They also visit local bazaars and flea markets, where they can find inexpensive clothes and accessories and vintage records and CDs. These teens, as well as those with less spending money, play outdoor sports together, do homework with each other, listen to music together, and stroll and relax in village plazas and city parks. It is a common sight to see same-gender friends showing affection toward each other as they stroll around. Girls hold each other's hands, while boys walk with their arms around their buddies' shoulders or neck. As author Daniel Hernandez explains, "It is a completely sexless gesture, an expression of unfiltered affection between friends, a common display in Mexico."[36]

Both adult and young Mexicans value their friends almost as highly as they do their families. Adolescents and teens frequently form lifelong friendships with other members of their gender. Some groups of male friends develop such close bonds that they refer to each other as *cuates*, or "twin brothers." According to editors Tim L. Merrill and Ramón Miró in a study posted on the Library of Congress's Country Studies website:

> Cuate (from the Náhuatl word meaning twin brother) is used throughout Mexico to describe a special male friend or group of friends with whom one spends considerable leisure time and who can be trusted with intimate information. Cuate groups can include up to ten members who share common interests, who are bound by intense friendship and personal relations, and who commit themselves to assisting each other in case of need.[37]

These friends become part of each other's extended families and will often serve as godparents to each other's children.

When they are not spending time together, friends connect with each other by texting and instant messaging. Approximately 28 million Mexicans ages twelve to thirty-four have smartphones. They also stay in touch via social media. Mexico has the second largest number of social media users in Latin America. Over 12 million Mexicans use Twitter. And approximately 92 percent of Internet users in Mexico, or about 38 million people, are active on Facebook. Many of these social networkers are teens and adolescents. According to comScore, a company that measures consumer behavior worldwide, an estimated 33 percent of social media site visitors in Mexico are aged fifteen to twenty-four. Even teens who do not have Internet access at home can get online at Internet cafés that are located in most cities and larger towns.

"*Cuate* (from the Náhuatl word meaning twin brother) is used throughout Mexico to describe a special male friend or group of friends with whom one spends considerable leisure time and who can be trusted with intimate information."[37]

—Tim L. Merrill and Ramón Miró, editors of a study posted on the Library of Congress's Country Studies website

Dating

Dating is another way Mexican teens enjoy themselves. Dating practices in Mexico are similar to those in most industrialized countries. Youngsters date because it is fun, not

Teens in Mexico, like those in other countries all over the world, enjoy spending time with their friends. Mexicans of all ages tend to value their friends almost as highly as they do their family members.

necessarily to lead to marriage. Young people often become acquainted with each other at school or church. Many are introduced by friends or extended family members. Indeed, in some respects couples are not just dating each other but also each other's families. Dating couples are usually invited to each other's family gatherings and are expected to socialize and get along with everyone, old and young. In general, Mexican teens want to please their families. They therefore are apt to date someone who meets with their family's approval.

There is no set age for when Mexican teens start dating. Traditionally, girls are not considered ready to date until their fifteenth birthday. But as dating has become more about socializing and

Shopping in Mexico

Like young people throughout the world, Mexican teens like to go shopping. In urban areas, teens can visit large, modern shopping malls and elegant designer boutiques. They can also shop in large American chain stores like Walmart in most Mexican metropolitan areas.

There are also indoor and outdoor *mercados*, or markets, in almost every city, town, and village. In fact, open-air markets have been a part of Mexico since before the arrival of the Spanish. Mazes of stalls sell everything from food to live animals. Merchants also hawk toys, handicrafts, clothes, electronics, and leather goods, among a myriad of other items. Unlike shopping in traditional stores, bargaining is part of the fun of shopping in Mexico's markets. Shoppers are expected to haggle with vendors over prices, and even the youngest of shoppers are skilled at bargaining.

Mexico's markets are extremely busy places, filled with people, merchandise, color, and hundreds of different smells. They can also be quite noisy. Music blasts from stalls that sell CDs and old records and cassette tapes.

Some markets are huge, snaking for miles. Mexico City's largest food market, for example, covers over 800 acres (324 ha) and houses more than two thousand vendors. Shopping in such huge markets can be tiring, even for energetic youngsters. Most markets offer shoppers a chance to relax and recharge. Stalls with little tables and chairs or benches offer all types of prepared food and beverages.

having fun and less about marriage, many families ignore this tradition. In families that still follow this tradition, younger teens often go out in mixed-gender groups until they are old enough to go on individual dates.

It is customary for boys to take the initiative when it comes to dating. Usually, males invite females out and pay for everything. This is considered good manners. Most Mexican women would be surprised and possibly insulted if they were asked to split the bill. Where young people go on dates depends on their age, their locality, and the amount of money they have to spend. Going out for dinner, a movie, or dancing are popular activities. The legal drinking age in Mexico is eighteen, making clubs that serve alcohol off limits to younger teens. Other less costly destinations include strolling in a park or town plaza, attending a private party, going on a picnic, and attending a family barbeque, just to name a few popular choices. But no matter the destination or the cost of the date, when dating individuals like each other, they are not reserved about showing it. Public displays of affection are socially acceptable in Mexico. Couples do not hesitate to cuddle and kiss in public.

Goal!

Playing sports, attending sporting events, and watching games on television is another way young people have fun. Groups of friends, dating couples, and extended family members often attend sporting events together. They also like watching televised games. Soccer—or *fútbol*, as it is known in Mexico—is far and away the most popular sport. As Jesús Ramirez, the director of Cruz Azul, a Mexico City soccer academy where many of Mexico's professional athletes train, explains, "In Mexico, the passion for soccer is widespread. Men, women, children, they all follow soccer."[38]

Soccer is an essential part of Mexican life. Young Mexicans do not just follow the sport; they play it everywhere—in parks, vacant lots, dusty alleys, busy streets, and makeshift fields all over Mexico. As journalist Jason Margolis explains: "I went to Mexico City's Daniel Garza neighborhood, a working class part of town, to watch young boys play ball. . . . The boys play right next to the highway on a small concrete court papered over by synthetic turf that's peeling away. The field is surrounded by netting and barbed wire. Balls ricochet off the concrete walls and goals made of steel bars."[39]

In the past, soccer was considered a boy's game. But that is changing. Mexico has a women's national soccer team that represents the nation in international competitions. These athletes have inspired more and more young girls to take to the field. Today lots of adolescents and teens play on female youth, interscholastic, and local teams. According to Mexico's national women's team member Bianca Sierra, "The women's game is growing a ton in Mexico City. I really feel like we are role models

> "In Mexico, the passion for soccer is widespread. Men, women, children, they all follow soccer."[38]
>
> —Jesús Ramirez, director of Cruz Azul, a well-known Mexico City soccer academy

for young girls. I just try to be the best that I can be every day so that young girls can continue to look up to me and follow their dreams."[40]

Mexico also has a men's national team, which has qualified to play in the World Cup fifteen times. There are also many local teams, on which prospective soccer stars sharpen their skills. These are divided into four different levels, much like baseball's farm teams.

Soccer matches are broadcast live on two Mexican television networks. Getting together with friends and family to watch televised games is a big part of many social gatherings. Going out to see a game is also a major activity. Mexico boasts a number of large modern soccer stadiums, where matches are played before huge crowds. Mexico City's Azteca Stadium is the third largest in the world. It holds more than 105,000 people. It is home to Mexico's national soccer team, as well as Mexico City's local team, Club America.

Seeing a live match is an unforgettable experience. Mexican soccer fans are passionate about their favorite teams. During a match, the air crackles with intensity and the noise is incredible. An article on the International Federation of Association Football's website describes Azteca Stadium this way: "The bowl's signature roof traps and amplifies noise from the massive upper level, filling the air with high pitch shrieks and a deafening, cacophonous din to make the Mexico City landmark, and home to domestic giants Club America, one of the loudest stadiums anywhere."[41]

It is not unusual for fistfights to break out between fans of opposing local teams. But when the national team is playing, fans unite in their support. Indeed, for Mexicans of all ages, soccer is more than just a game; it is an important social institution. As an article on don Quijote, a Spanish-language-learning website, explains, "In Mexico . . . soccer is not only a sport but a passion, part of their culture, national identity and pastime."[42]

Professional Wrestling, Mexican Style

Watching professional wrestling matches—or *lucha libre* (free fight), as it is known in Mexico—whether televised or live is another fun activity that young Mexicans enjoy. The sport, which originated in Mexico, is a mix of traditional Greco-Roman wres-

Teens play a pick-up game of soccer in Mexico City. Soccer is the most popular sport in Mexico—a passion shared by men, women, teens, and children alike.

tling, high-flying acrobatics, martial arts, and theater. It is famous for the colorful masks that the wrestlers (male, female, and transvestites dressed in drag) wear.

Masks played an important role in ancient Aztec rituals. Their use by Mexican wrestlers pays tribute to the nation's history. Each wrestler adopts a character or persona in the ring. The masks, which evoke images of ancient heroes, gods, and fierce animals, help define that persona. Indeed, a wrestler's mask is considered so important that fully removing an opponent's mask during a match is grounds for disqualification.

Fans identify wrestlers by their masks. In fact, many wrestlers keep their real identity secret. They are known only by their wrestling personas—and even make public appearances in their masks. One of Mexico's most beloved wrestlers, El Santo, was even buried wearing his mask.

Wrestlers are categorized into two distinct groups: *tecnicos*, or good guys; and *rudos*, or villains. *Tecnicos* fight clean, act honorably, and are seen as champions of justice; many are also spokespeople for social causes. *Rudos*, on the other hand, fight dirty and act dishonorably. Youthful fans love to hate them.

Matches are quite a spectacle. There may be as many as six wrestlers in the ring at the same time. Most come from family groups that form wrestling teams. Children in these families start training for the sport almost as soon as they can walk, and they make their professional debuts in their mid-teens. Most establish a fan base by performing in village plazas. As they become famous, they move up to large arenas that seat thousands of fans.

Mexican wrestlers are idolized by children, teens, and adults. Comic books, trading cards, posters, movies, video games, and animated television series portray wrestling characters much like superheroes. Wrestling masks and action figures are favorite children's toys. For older fans, there are lucha libre–inspired energy drinks, jewelry, clothing, and athletic shoes, among other merchandise. Donovan Garcia, who grew up in Mexico and now lives in California, recalls the role the sport played in his youth. "This is part of the culture. . . . Family, music, lucha libre and futbol. That's all there was."[43]

Other Popular Sports

Charreada or *charrería* (rodeo), a sport similar to American rodeo, is another distinctive Mexican sport that youngsters enjoy. The sport developed during Spanish colonial times from informal contests in which ranch hands showed off their skills by competing against ranch hands, or *charros*, from neighboring ranches. Modern charreadas are formal events with strict rules.

Charreadas are held in outdoor arenas located throughout Mexico. The rodeos last about three hours and consist of a total of nine riding and roping events involving men and one precision riding event involving women. Participants compete as teams made up of family groups. Most of these families have been involved in the sport for generations. Children in these families start training for the sport as soon as they can sit on a horse. Participants wear ornate costumes that consist of short boots with metal spurs, close-fitting jackets, leather vests, chaps over pants, and wide-brimmed hats, all of which are decorated with intricate embroidery and silver studs. Individual team members are scored for each event based on their grace and skill. These scores are tallied to determine the winning team.

Winners do not get a monetary prize. But they do get public acclaim. Their discipline, courage, and dedication to their family team serves as a source of pride for Mexicans, as well as a reminder of the traditions and values of rural life in colonial Mexico. As Raúl E. Gaona, a charro and historian, explains, "Anyone can be a good horseman. It just takes practice. But that's not what charrería is about. Some belong only to compete in the arena,

Participants in a charreada wave to the crowd. Charreadas are events similar to the rodeos held in the United States and showcase horsemanship skills, including roping and riding, that have been passed down for generations.

but that's not being a charro. Charrería is a way of life outside the arena as well as in. It's family and social traditions and culture."[44]

Because the sport embodies what many people consider to be some of the best aspects of traditional Mexican culture, it is very popular with families. It is not unusual to see parents, grandparents, children, and teens out together enjoying the show. And it is quite a show, beginning with the opening ceremony in which the smartly dressed participants parade around the arena on horseback in perfect synchronization, accompanied by the lively music of a mariachi band. The band also plays before and after each event. And when the rodeo ends, it is usually followed by a large fiesta held in the town plaza, complete with food, drink, music, and dancing. Dating couples, groups of friends, and multigenerational family groups mix and mingle at these fiestas, which can last late into the night.

> "Charrería is a way of life outside the arena as well as in. It's family and social traditions and culture."[44]
>
> —Raúl E. Gaona, historian and charro

Music and Dance

The mariachi bands that play at charreadas are beloved by Mexicans of all ages. Music plays a large role in Mexican life and culture, and listening and dancing to music are activities that Mexican teens enjoy. It is a common sight to see teens walking through city streets wearing earbuds or headphones.

Mexican youths are exposed to diverse forms of music. Some of their favorite sounds are popular throughout the Western world, while other sounds are distinctly Mexican. Like teens in most of the Western world, Mexican youngsters like modern hit tunes. They flock to concerts in the nation's cities to see American and European rock, pop, heavy metal, and hip-hop groups. For instance, in 2016 superstars like Adele, Justin Bieber, Guns N' Roses, Selena Gomez, and Black Sabbath, just to name a few, played to huge crowds in Mexico. Homegrown Mexican rock, hip-hop, heavy metal, and pop bands that perform in Spanish are also wildly popular. Electronic music is trendy, too. On Friday and Saturday nights, dance clubs in major cities and resort areas are packed with young people moving to the electronic beats that DJs spin.

Controversial Music

Corrido music is popular with many young Mexicans. Corridos are songs written about significant events taking place at the time the songs were written. The earliest of these songs describes the battles of the Mexican revolution of 1910, as well as the feats of revolutionary heroes like Pancho Villa and Emilio Zapata.

Modern corridos center on more current themes. Some tell about the lives of undocumented Mexican immigrants in the United States. Other corridos, known as *narcocorridos*, tell stories about, and often glorify, illegal drug trafficking. These songs, which have been compared to American gangster rap, are popular with many Mexican teens. But they are controversial. Typically, the lyrics describe actual places, dates, events, and people related to the drug trade. Most seem to glorify the violence associated with drug trafficking and show approval of illegal activities.

Some Mexican radio stations have banned certain narcocorridos from airplay. But many young people listen to these songs and download them from the Internet. And bootleg copies of the songs are sold at Mexican flea markets.

Young Mexicans also listen and dance to more traditional music like mariachi that reflects Mexican history and culture. Mariachi music originated in southern Mexico during the nineteenth century and combines native Mexican and European musical forms. Mariachi bands are made up of five or more musicians singing and playing violins, trumpets, and two uniquely Mexican instruments—a large, deep-sounding guitar known as a *guitarrón* and a small, five-string guitar known as a *vihuela*. The musical rhythms vary depending on the song. Most are full of fun and energy. The lyrics of mariachi songs tell stories that depict the essence of Mexican culture—love, family, friendship, machismo, and rural life. The songs are Mexico's own folk tunes. Even young children know the words of many mariachi songs.

Mariachi songs are often sentimental. Hiring a mariachi band to sing to a girlfriend is considered very romantic. It is also traditional for well-to-do teens and adolescents to hire a mariachi band to serenade their mothers outside her bedroom window on Mother's Day morning. And weddings, baptisms, and big parties are not complete without a mariachi band.

Indeed, mariachi musicians dressed in traditional charro suits can be found all over Mexico. They stroll from table to table in restaurants and cafés, taking requests from patrons who reward them with a monetary tip. On Sundays as many as four thousand mariachi players fill Mexico City's Garibaldi Plaza, where they take requests from passersby and network with locals in hopes of soliciting future gigs.

Mariachi music is so much a part of Mexican life that many young people take private music lessons to learn to play mariachi style. And music classes in many schools include mariachi bands. The music is part of Mexico's cultural identity. It serves as a link between multiple generations, and for Mexican adolescents and teens it is synonymous with fun and celebration.

CHAPTER FIVE

Religious Influences

Approximately 82 percent of all Mexicans identify as Catholic, giving Mexico the second-highest number of Catholic residents in the world. However, not all Mexican Catholics attend church regularly. In fact, it is estimated that only 3 percent of Mexican Catholics attend daily Mass, while 44 percent attend at least once a week. Nor do all Mexican Catholics uniformly agree with all of the church's teachings. This is especially true when it comes to conservative doctrine concerning human sexuality. As a result, many Mexican teens and adults tend to pick and choose which Catholic principles they practice. For example, a 2014 survey by the Pew Research Center found that even though the Catholic Church condemns homosexuality and gay marriage, about half of all Mexican Catholics think gay marriage should be legal. Even fewer Mexican Catholics think that other behaviors related to pre-marital sex, artificial birth control, and divorce, which the church sees as sinful, are morally wrong. According to the survey, 66 percent of Mexican Catholics say the church should allow contraceptive use, and 60 percent say divorce is acceptable. Indeed, for many young Mexicans, religion is more closely tied to traditions and customs passed down by their parents than with actual religious doctrine and practices.

Mexicans have a long history of not taking church doctrine literally or rigidly adhering to church practices. "Ignoring what the priests tell us is part of the history of Mexico,"[45] explains Maria de la Luz Estrada, a reproductive rights activist with the Mexico City–based group Catholics for the Right to Choose. Mexico's ancient people practiced their own religion. Many did not convert to Catholicism without a fight. As converts, they neither accepted all of the church's teachings nor discarded all aspects of their former faiths. Instead, they blended their ancient beliefs and customs into their new religion, creating a unique view of the Catholicism that allowed individuals to accept certain aspects of the faith while rejecting others.

Nevertheless, Catholic beliefs and customs play a prominent role in Mexican culture and impact the lives of young people growing up here. As Vanessa Barajas, a teen of Mexican heritage, explains, "I grew up with Catholic laws that somewhat shaped who I am. Things like don't steal, respect your parents, and forgiveness."[46]

Premarital Sex and Teen Pregnancy

Although Catholic doctrine prohibits sex outside of marriage, many young Mexicans disregard church teaching on this issue. About 31 percent of Mexican teens ages fifteen to nineteen are sexually active, according to the National Survey of Health and Nutrition (ENSN) conducted by the Mexican government. Of the sexually active teens surveyed, 66 percent reported using some type of contraceptive, while 32.4 percent said they do not use any form of birth control. There are a number of reasons why these youngsters do not practice birth control. Due to their religious beliefs, some plan not to have sexual intercourse. When they do so anyway, they are not prepared to use protection. In fact, according to a 2013 report by the United Nations Population Fund (UNFPA), 80 percent of adolescent and teen couples in Mexico did not use a contraceptive during their first sexual encounter.

Mexican students receive sex education beginning in upper primary school. And birth control pills and condoms can be purchased over the counter in Mexican pharmacies. Other contraceptives, including the "morning-after" emergency contraceptive pill, can be obtained at government-run health clinics. The morning-after pill is available, despite opposition by church officials, who argue that it is abortive and should therefore be banned. This stance keeps many teens who have unprotected sex from using the drug.

With almost a third of sexually active young people not using birth control, teen pregnancy rates are alarmingly high in Mexico. The UNFPA reports that Mexico is the leading nation in teen pregnancy, with 64.2 teen pregnancies per thousand births. And the ENSN survey found that of the sexually active young people ages twelve to nineteen responding to the survey, 51.9 percent have been pregnant at least once. The average age for pregnancy is sixteen; however, according to the UNFPA report, 23 percent of sexually active girls ages ten to fourteen in Mexico have been pregnant.

Teen pregnancy is associated with a number of negative consequences. In Latin America girls under age fifteen are four times more likely to die in childbirth than females in their twenties, and babies born to younger mothers are at risk of having serious health issues. Moreover, teen pregnancy increases the probability of young parents, and especially young mothers, dropping out of school. Without an education, it is difficult for teen parents to find stable employment. Consequently, they and their children are likely to live in poverty.

For many young Mexicans, religion is more closely tied to tradition than to actual religious doctrine and practices. One example is the annual three-day-long horseback pilgrimage to the mountaintop shrine of Cristo Rey in Guanajuato (pictured).

Turning to Other Faiths

Although the majority of Mexicans identify as Catholic, it is not the only religion that is practiced in Mexico. Mexican law provides for freedom of religion. Approximately 14 million belong to Protestant Christian denominations, and a lower number practice Judaism, Islam, and other Eastern religions.

Some of these individuals were born into these religions. However, some young Mexicans have chosen to leave the Catholic faith for Pentecostal and other charismatic Christian faiths. This is especially true for those living in southern states that border Guatemala, a country with a large number of Protestants. Indeed, the number of Protestants and Evangelical Christians in Mexico has increased from 1.28 percent of the population in 1950 to almost 8 percent of the total population in 2010. This figure does not include Jehovah's Witnesses or Mormons, two groups that are also seeing many new converts.

According to Mexican sociologist and historian Roberto Blancarte, between 2000 and 2010 approximately 4 million Mexican Catholics left the Catholic Church. Although many have converted to other religions, many young Mexicans profess to have no religion. Experts do not know why so many Mexicans are turning away from Catholicism; however, it is possible that conservative church doctrine has negatively affected these individuals' faith. As Blancarte explains, "As long as the church . . . representatives remain unconnected to people's needs and keep slamming the use of contraceptives and condoms and saying that sex education is bad, more and more people will leave."

Quoted in Julian Rodriguez Marin, "More than 1,000 Mexicans Leave Catholic Church Daily, Expert Says," *Latin American Herald Tribune*. www.laht.com.

Abortion

In an effort to end an unwanted pregnancy, some young women seek an abortion. Abortion rights are controversial in Mexico. Catholic doctrine, which says that life begins at conception, prohibits the procedure. The Mexican constitution provides for the separation of church and state, and the federal government generally respects this right. Laws concerning abortion, however, fall under the jurisdiction of individual state governments, most of which are strongly influenced by church doctrine prohibiting abortion. As of 2016, abortion is legal in Mexico City. According to the law, any woman who is no more than twelve weeks pregnant can get an abortion there, no matter the reason for the procedure.

However, health care professionals in the capital can legally refuse to administer an abortion because of their faith, which lessens the availability of the procedure.

For Mexico City residents, abortion services are free in public hospitals. Women from other states are charged a fee. These women travel to Mexico City because abortion is illegal in the rest of the nation. In fact, after abortion became legal in the capital in 2007, many states passed fetal rights laws stating that life begins at conception, in keeping with Catholic doctrine. Based on these laws, outside of the federal district, women are subject to criminal prosecution for having an abortion, except under limited circumstances. All states permit the procedure in cases of rape. If the mother's life is in danger, abortion is permitted in all but three states—Guerrero, Guanajuato, and Queretaro. It is also permitted in eighteen states in cases of severe fetal deformities. However, with the exception of the federal district, almost no state health facilities provide access to the procedure, no matter the circumstances. This makes it almost impossible for young women to get an abortion unless they travel to Mexico City. Many teens cannot afford the cost of traveling to the capital in order to access a legal abortion. As a result, some ingest dangerous drugs in an attempt to induce a miscarriage, or they seek unsafe clandestine abortions. These procedures result in about two thousand deaths per year, making illegal abortions the fifth leading cause of maternal death in Mexico. Moreover, if a young woman suffering from a botched back-alley abortion goes to a hospital outside of Mexico City, health care workers are required to report suspicion of an illegal abortion to the police. As a study by the Mexico City–based Group on Reproductive Choice explains, "There have been very important advances, like the decriminalization of abortion in Mexico City up to 12 weeks of gestation. . . . However, general reforms to protect prenatal life without considering the protection of the life of the mother in question have negatively impacted the access to legal abortion services and safety throughout the country."[47]

Young Mexicans are divided about abortion rights. The ENSN survey found that 48 percent of teens who responded to the survey approve of abortion only when the mother's life is at risk, 42.7 percent say it is acceptable if the pregnancy is a product of rape, and 41.7 percent approve of the procedure in cases of severe fetal abnormalities.

Homosexuality and Gay Marriage

Young homosexuals in Mexico face other issues. In 2015 Mexico's Supreme Court ruled that state laws that define marriage as a union between a man and a woman are discriminatory and unconstitutional. This ruling essentially legalized same-sex marriage in all Mexican states. However, few states perform the ceremonies. The only place in the nation that does perform them is Mexico City, which legalized gay marriage in 2009. In an effort to force states to comply with the ruling, in 2016 Mexican president Enrique Peña Nieto proposed federal constitutional reform legalizing same-sex marriage throughout Mexico. This was met by thousands of people throughout the country demonstrating in protest of such reform.

These demonstrations were organized by religious groups. Catholic doctrine prohibits homosexual behavior and gay marriage. Homosexuality, according to Bishop Leopoldo Gonzalez of Guadalajara, Mexico, "goes against nature. . . . The position of the Church is never going to change. . . . In order to grow healthily, we need a paternal figure and a maternal figure."[48]

> "Like every other big city, like New York or like Los Angeles, you have all sorts of people and there's so much diversity, which makes it okay to be gay here in the city."[50]
>
> —Eli Nassau of Guimel, a Mexico City LGBT Jewish group

Such doctrine influences the way many Mexicans treat homosexuals. According to the ENSN survey, 51.9 percent of homosexual teens respondents felt that their rights were not respected on some occasions due to their sexual identity. Pedro Siordia Mora, a twenty-three-year-old gay man, explains what happened to him when he and his boyfriend kissed in a bar in Guadalajara during a New Year's Eve celebration: "The security guards told us that it wasn't a gay bar and that we had to leave."[49]

Moreover, some young gays feel they must keep their sexual preferences hidden out of fear of being rejected by loved ones. Yet despite the church's strong influence, attitudes are gradually changing—especially in Mexico City, where it is not unusual to see young same-sex couples holding hands and openly embracing. As Eli Nassau of Guimel, a Mexico City LGBT Jewish group, explains, "Like every other big city, like New York or like Los Angeles, you have all sorts

Our Lady of Guadalupe: A National Symbol

Although not all young Mexicans are devoted Catholics, 79.1 percent of adolescents and teens responding to the Mexican government's ENSN survey said that they believe in the Virgin of Guadalupe. The Virgin of Guadalupe is a Catholic title for the Virgin Mary, the mother of Jesus Christ. She is the patron saint of Mexico. Pictures of her can be found in almost every Mexican home.

According to legend, the Virgin miraculously appeared on a hillside in Mexico City before an indigenous Mexican peasant in 1531. Speaking in Nahuatl, his native language, she told him that she was the mother of all Mexicans and asked him to build a church on the site in her honor. As she requested, a church was built on the site. That church is the most visited Catholic pilgrimage site in the Americas and the third most visited site in the world. Every year, hundreds of thousands of Mexicans travel to the church on the anniversary of her appearance. Many trek hundreds of miles on foot. Some enter the church on their knees. Among these pilgrims are thousands of young people. After making their way to the church , many camp out in local parks, where they eat, drink, sing songs to the Virgin, and celebrate the occasion and their journey.

of people and there's so much diversity, which makes it okay to be gay here in the city."[50]

Rites of Passage

Whether or not young Mexicans accept all of the church's teachings, for historic reasons religious traditions play a big role in Mexican culture. Religious holidays are widely celebrated throughout the country. And from birth to death, most rites of passage in a young person's life are associated with Catholicism. For instance, to introduce them into the faith, infants are baptized in a traditional church ceremony, which is usually followed by a big celebration. Coco, a blogger and the daughter of Mexican immigrants now living in the United States, explains, "My family is from Mexico, where a Baptism is an important religious event. . . . We follow the religious ceremony with a special party, just like in Mexico. We invite our close friends and family for a big meal, complete with a mariachi band."[51]

At eight years old, most children receive their First Holy Communion. During this ceremony, children receive the sacrament of the Holy Eucharist for the first time. This sacrament, which involves eating a blessed wafer and taking a sip of wine, symbolizes the body and blood of Jesus Christ. The ritual is considered one of the most important occasions in a Catholic's life. To prepare for it, children attend hour-long, weekly classes for two years, in which they are instructed in all the prayers related to the Catholic Mass. Most first communions are done in large groups. The girls wear frilly white dresses and a little tiara, and the boys wear suits and ties. The church ceremony is usually followed by a party, which, depending on the family's income, may be a family dinner or an elaborate affair with food, music, dancing, and games for the children. Al Barrus, an American who lives in Mexico, describes such an event:

> After the kids took their wafer and sip of wine, the communion party headed to a very fancy country-club garden. While it was only 11 a.m. there was booze for the adults and bouncy castles for the children. . . . There were boxes of dress-up clothes so you could look like a clown. Girls could get manicures and pedicures. Face painters were painting faces. There was a pony there too.[52]

A few years later (usually at age twelve or thirteen), young boys and girls receive their confirmation. This religious ceremony serves as a renewal and affirmation of the youngster and his or her family's faith. Traditionally, before being confirmed, Mexican children must pass a test based on their continuing weekly religious studies. As with almost all Mexican events, the ceremony is followed by a family gathering and party.

Another rite of passage associated with Catholicism celebrates a fifteen-year-old girl's transition from girlhood to womanhood, and her loyalty and commitment to God and family. This festive event is known as a *quince años* or *quinceañera* (fifteenth-birthday celebration). The celebration begins with a religious ceremony known as a Thanksgiving Mass. The celebrant arrives in church accompanied by her parents, godparents, and court of honor. The latter typically consists of the birthday girl's closest friends, siblings, and cousins, paired off into couples. During the Mass, the birthday girl renews her commitment to her faith. According to authors Andrea Lawson Gray and Adriana Almazan

Lahl, "The girl prays to God in order to renew her baptismal commitment, to strengthen her faith, to ask for strength as she enters a new phase in life, to give thanks for arriving at age fifteen, and to honor her parents."[53]

As part of the ritual, her parents and godparents present her with a number of symbolic gifts that have been blessed by the priest. These include a rosary and a bible; a tiara that denotes her as a princess of God; a ring that symbolizes her unending faith; and a bouquet of flowers, which the young lady leaves on the altar as an offering to the Virgin of Guadalupe.

The church ceremony is followed by a celebratory reception and dance, which usually take place at the young lady's home or

Teens participate in a Mass as part of their quinceañera, *or fifteenth-birthday celebration, in Juarez. This rite of passage symbolically marks a girl's transition from girlhood to womanhood.*

in a banquet facility. The reception is an elegant dress-up event that includes lots of food and drink, music, special toasts, a first dance performed by the honoree and her father, and choreographed dance routines performed by the young lady and members of her court. As Lahl recalls:

> I attended quinceaneras in . . . large patios with buffet style Mexican cazuela [stew], as well as a few in fancy salons at well-known hotels with decorated tables and exquisite food; some of these were more elegant venues than some weddings I have been to. At these the dresses were handmade with intricate embroidery and the chambelanes [male members of the court of honor] wore tuxedos. Others were not as opulent but they were always a dress-up affair, with de [rigueur] cocktail dresses for the ladies and suits and ties for the gentlemen.[54]

Whether elaborate or modest, the religious ceremony and the ensuing celebration, is, according to writer and bilingual educator Stephen Saylor, "traditionally one of the most sacred and sentimental times in a young girl's life."[55]

Life, Death, and Celebration

Like rites of passage, most Mexican holidays have religious roots. Some holidays, like Christmas and Easter, are celebrated by Christians throughout the world. Others, like the Day of the Dead, are more unusual, reflecting the way Mexicans combine Amerindian beliefs with Catholicism. During the holiday, which is usually celebrated from October 30 to November 2, Mexicans honor dead loved ones. The celebration combines aspects of Catholicism's All Saints Day, which memorializes deceased saints, with an Aztec festival known as the Feast of the Dead. As Mexican writer Rommel Cesena explains, "It is a beautiful tradition that honors our ancestors, and exemplifies how the clash of two worlds—the white European and the Native American, or 'Indian'—can produce something of real beauty and complexity."[56]

Day of the Dead is an important holiday intended to honor deceased forebears, and reinforces the concept that life and death are inseparable. Here, teens dressed as skeletons march in a Day of the Dead parade.

The holiday begins with families building colorful little altars in their homes in memory of dead loved ones whose spirits are believed to return to earth at midnight on November 2. The altars usually contain photos of the deceased, objects that were important to the person, rosaries, religious candles, flowers, and special skull-shaped bread and candy. On the night of November 1, families gather in cemeteries throughout the nation. They have picnics on the graves of their loved ones, where they place baskets of the returning souls' favorite foods. As part of the festivities they reminisce about the departed and the good times they shared, and they serenade the dead with their favorite songs.

Although the celebration may sound morbid to non-Mexicans, it helps shape the way Mexican adolescents and teens view death. Most Mexicans believe that life and death are inseparable. By memorializing the dead, they feel that they are keeping a part of the dead alive until they are reunited in the afterlife. As Cesena explains, "While many cultures fear death and mortality, Mexicans see its beauty, and have a strong, even romantic connection to it. I once read that 'it's wrong to say you don't have a family: Even if they are all dead, you still have them.' For me, this captures the warm relationship we Mexicans have with death."[57]

Clearly, whether in the form of celebrations, holidays, and rites of passage or concerns about church teachings related to human sexuality, the Catholic faith plays a large role in Mexican culture and traditions. It also has a significant place in the lives of the nation's adolescents and teens.

SOURCE NOTES

Chapter One: A Nation of Contrasts

1. Arena Barrientos, "What Is It Like to Grow Up in Juarez?," Quora, October 27, 2011. www.quora.com.
2. Quoted in Daniel Hernandez, *Down & Delirious in Mexico City*. New York: Scribner, 2011, p. 17.
3. Quoted in Alasdair Baverstock, "'I Sell My Body to Perverts to Make a Dollar': Mexico City's Homeless 'Rat Children' Who Sleep in SEWERS and Sniff Glue to Forget the 'Horrible' Things They Have to Do for Food," *Daily Mail* (London), November 11, 2015. www.dailymail.co.uk.
4. Hernandez, *Down & Delirious in Mexico City*, p. 95.
5. Jim Phypers and Mindy Phypers, "Day-to-Day Life in Our Village in Rural Veracruz, Mexico," Solar Haven, 2013. http://mexico.solarhaven.org.
6. Carol M. Merchasin, *This Is Mexico*. Berkeley, CA: She Writes, 2015, p. 96.
7. Quoted in *PBS NewsHour*, "In Mexico, a Plan to Beat Poverty with Health Care and Education," December 29, 2009. www.pbs.org.

Chapter Two: Family: The Heart of Mexico

8. Quoted in Stan Gotlieb, "A Tale of Two Students," *Mexconnect,* 2008. www.mexconnect.com.
9. Merchasin, *This Is Mexico*, p. 152.
10. Marcelina Hardy, "Cultural Differences of Teenagers," Love to Know. http://teens.lovetoknow.com.
11. Amy Kirkcaldy, "Mamitis in Mexico," *Mexconnect*, 2008. www.mexconnect.com.
12. Roberto Campa-Mada, "Mexico," in *Teen Life in Latin America & the Caribbean*, ed. Cynthia Margarita Tompkins and Kristen Sternberg. Westport, CT: Greenwood, 2004, p. 243.

13. Quoted in Merchasin, *This Is Mexico*, p. 143.
14. Hernandez, *Down & Delirious in Mexico City*, p. 23.
15. Campa-Mada, "Mexico," p. 244.
16. Quoted in Annenberg Learner, "A Day in the Life of a Mexican Student." www.learner.org.
17. Merchasin, *This Is Mexico*, p. 116.
18. Quoted in Sara Miller Llana, "Mexico Considers 'Ban' on Street Children," *Christian Science Monitor*, June 1, 2009. www.csmonitor.com.
19. Maria Jose Cespedes, "Sobremesa in Mexico City," *Localist*, December 22, 2014. http://thelocalist.com.
20. Rommel Cesena, "Sundays, Family and Revolution," *Localist*, September 28, 2013. http://thelocalist.com.

Chapter Three: School and Work
21. Quoted in Laurie M. Scott, "Back to School Around the World," *Christian Science Monitor*, September 4, 2001. www.csmonitor.com.
22. Campa-Mada, "Mexico," p. 250.
23. H. James McLaughlin, "Schooling in Mexico: A Brief Guide for U.S. Educators," ERIC Digests, 2016. www.ericdigests.org.
24. McLaughlin, "Schooling in Mexico."
25. Laura Winfree, "USA vs Mexico: Education," *Gringation Cancun* (blog), November 14, 2012. http://gringationcancun.com.
26. Laura Winfree, "How to Halfway Graduate from a Mexican University," *Gringation Cancun* (blog), October 26, 2012. http://gringationcancun.com.
27. Quoted in Richard Marosi, "In Mexico's Fields, Children Toil to Harvest Crops That Make It to the American Table," *Los Angeles Times*, December 14, 2014. http://graphics.latimes.com.
28. Merchasin, *This Is Mexico*, p. 124.
29. Quoted in Codie Sanchez, "Stranded on the Border," Walter Cronkite School of Journalism and Mass Communication, February 16, 2014. https://issuu.com.
30. Quoted in Sanchez, "Stranded on the Border."

31. Quoted in Lulu Garcia-Navarro, "Vendors Drive Mexico's 'Informal' Economy," NPR, June 13, 2006. www.npr.org.

32. Quoted in Clayton Conn, "Informal Economy Makes Up 26% of Mexico's GDP," teleSUR, August 8, 2014. www.telesurtv .net.

33. Quoted in Duncan Tucker, "Parking Cars on the Edge of Mexico's Informal Economy," Al Jazeera, April 24, 2016. www .aljazeera.com.

34. Quoted in Sanchez, "Stranded on the Border."

35. Quoted in Sanchez, "Stranded on the Border."

Chapter Four: Social Life

36. Hernandez, *Down & Delirious in Mexico City*, p. 9.

37. Tim L. Merrill and Ramón Miró, eds., "Interpersonal Relations," Country Studies, Library of Congress. http://countrystudies .us.

38. Quoted in Jason Margolis, "If Mexican Boys Dominate Global Youth Soccer, Why Don't They Grow Up to Win the World Cup?," PRI, June 12, 2014. www.pri.org.

39. Margolis, "If Mexican Boys Dominate Global Youth Soccer, Why Don't They Grow Up to Win the World Cup?"

40. Quoted in Kevin Baxter, "Women's Soccer in Mexico Growing with Help from U.S. Players," *Los Angeles Times*, May 16, 2015. www.latimes.com.

41. FIFA, "Estadio Azteca, Mexico City." www.fifa.com.

42. Don Quijote, "Mexican Soccer." www.donquijote.org.

43. Quoted in Kevin Baxter, "Lucha Libre Gives Fans a Taste of the Homeland," SFGate, March 22, 2009. www.sfgate.com.

44. Quoted in Wendy Devlin, "Charreada in Guadalajara," *Mexconnect*. www.mexconnect.com.

Chapter Five: Religious Influences

45. Quoted in Marion Lloyd, "Mexico Adds Sex to School Syllabus," *Houston Chronicle*, August 22, 2006. www.chron.com.

46. Quoted in Alejandra Aguilera, "#GrowingUpLatina," Latinitas, October 23, 2015. http://laslatinitas.com.

47. Quoted in Kari Paul, "The Criminalization of Abortion Continues in Mexico," *Ms.*, May 30, 2013. http://msmagazine.com.
48. Quoted in Duncan Tucker, "Mexico's Gay Rights Movement Gaining Ground," Al Jazeera, January 24, 2014. www.aljazeera.com.
49. Quoted in Tucker, "Mexico's Gay Rights Movement Gaining Ground."
50. Quoted in Michael K. Lavers, "It's Okay to Be Gay in Mexico City," *Washington Blade* (Washington, DC), January 5, 2015. www.washingtonblade.com.
51. Coco, "Mexican Baptism Traditions," *Coco's Blog*, VidaCoco.com, August 12, 2011. www.vidacoco.com.
52. Al Barrus, "First Communion in Mexico: A Rite of Passage," *Mexpro* (blog), May 29, 2013. www.mexpro.com.
53. Andrea Lawson Gray and Adriana Almazan Lahl, *Celebraciones Mexicanas: History, Traditions, and Recipes*. Lanham, MD: AltaMira, 2013, p. 294.
54. Gray and Lahl, *Celebraciones Mexicanas*, p. 296.
55. Stephen Saylor, "Mexican Quinceanera Traditions," Our Everyday Life, 2016. http://oureverydaylife.com.
56. Rommel Cesena, "Death, a Day in Mexico," *Localist*, November 2013. http://thelocalist.com.
57. Cesena, "Death, a Day in Mexico."

FOR FURTHER RESEARCH

Books

A.M. Buckley, *Mexico*. Edina, MN: Abdo, 2012.

Michael Centore, *Mexico: Tradition, Culture, and Daily Life*. Broomall, PA: Mason Crest, 2015.

Margaret Haerens, *Mexico's Drug War*. Farmington Hills, MI: Greenhaven, 2013.

Colleen Madonna and Flood Williams, *Spirit of a Nation: The People of Mexico*. Broomall, PA: Mason Crest, 2014.

Erica M. Stokes, *Victoria! The Sports of Mexico*. Broomall, PA: Mason Crest, 2014.

Internet Sources

Central Intelligence Agency, "*The World Factbook*: North America; Mexico," 2016. www.cia.gov/library/publications/the-world -factbook/geos/mx.html.

History, "History of Mexico," 2016. www.history.com/topics/mex ico/history-of-mexico.

Jessica Magaziner and Carlos Monroy, "Education in Mexico," *World Education News & Review*, August 16, 2016. http://wenr .wes.org/2016/08/education-in-mexico.

OECD Better Life Index, "Mexico," 2015. www.oecdbetterlifein dex.org/countries/mexico.

Websites

Facts About Mexico (www.facts-about-mexico.com/index.html). This website provides information about Mexico's history, culture, people, food, and religion.

Localist (http://thelocalist.com). The *Localist* is an online travel and culture magazine. All the articles are written by natives of the country featured in the article. It has a large section on Mexico covering a wide range of topics.

Mexconnect (www.mexconnect.com). *Mexconnect* is an online magazine devoted to providing information about life in Mexico. It contains thousands of articles and photos on a variety of topics.

Mexico Cooks! (http://mexicocooks.typepad.com/mexico_cooks). Mexico Cooks! provides information about Mexican holidays, culture, religion, sports, markets, and food. It includes lots of pictures and recipes.

Traditional Mexican Culture (www.traditional-mexican-culture .com). This website provides articles on Mexican culture, food, religion, art, history, holidays, and more.

INDEX

Note: Boldface page numbers indicate illustrations

abortion, 58–59

All Saint's Day, 64

Aztecan civilization, 10

Azteca Stadium (Mexico City), 48

baptism, 22, 53, 61

Barajas, Vanessa, 55–56

Barrus, Al, 62

biodiversity, 9

birth control, 55
  percentage of teens using, 56

Blancarte, Roberto, 58

Border Patrol, US, 40, **41**

Camarena, Jonathan Fonseca, 32

Campa-Mada, Roberto, 22, 26, 27, 32–33

Castillo, Alejandrina, 37–38

Catholic Church, 58
  adherence to doctrines of, 55–56

festivals of, 64–66

rites of passage in, 61–64

Cesena, Rommel, 30, 64, 66

Cespedes, Maria Jose, 28–29

charreadas (rodeos), 50–52, **51**

CIA World Factbook, 27

climate, 9

corrido music, 53

Cortés, Hernán, 10

crime, 12

Cristo Rey shrine pilgrimage (Guanajuato), **57**

cuate, 44

dating, 44–47

Day of the Dead, 64–66, **65**

diet, 25–26

Don/Doña, 25

drug trade, 12

education
  higher, 35–36
  national curriculum, 33–35

private, 32–33

public, 31–32

See also schools

Ek Balam (Mayan architectural site), **10**

emigration, to US, reasons for, 40–42

employment

in high-tech industries, 36–37

in informal economy, 40

in *maquiladoras*, 38–39

families/family life

extended, 22–23

housekeeping responsibilities, 26–28

leisure activities, 28–30

meals, 25–26

names and, 23

nuclear, 19–21

family names, 23

First Holy Communion, 61–62

Franco, Hugo, 38–39

Fuentes, Neftali, 38

Gaona, Raúl E., 51–52

Garcia, Donovan, 50

gay marriage, 60

support for legalization of, 55

geography, 8–9

Gonzalez, Leopoldo, 60

government, **7**, 16

Gray, Andrea Lawson, 62–63

Group on Reproductive Choice, 59

Guadalupe, Virgin of, 61

Guanajuato, **24**

Hernandez, Daniel, 14, 24, 43

Hidalgo, Mary Lou, 40

holidays, 11

Day of the Dead, 64–66, **65**

homes/housing, 23

rural, **15**, 25

urban, **24**, 24–25

immigration, illegal, 41

income inequality, 18

indigenous people, 17

industry/industries, **7**

information resources, 71–72

Internet, number of users of, **7**

Lahl, Adriana Almazan, 62–63, 64

language, **7**, 11

leisure activities, 28–30

literacy, **7**

lucha libre (professional wrestling), 48–50

Luz Estrada, Maria de la, 55

maquiladoras, 38–39
  sexual discrimination in, 39

Margolis, Jason, 47

mariachi music, 52–54

Mayan civilization, 10

McLaughlin, H. James, 33, 34, 35

Merchasin, Carol M., 17, 19, 28, 38

Merrill, Tim L., 43–44

Mexico
  economic inequality in, 17–18
  facts about, **7**
  flag of, **6**
  geography of, 8–9
  government of, 16
  history of, 10–11
  map of, **6**

Mexico City, **13**
  subway in, 13–14

military service, 34

minimum wage, 38

Miró, Ramón, 43–44

Mora, Pedro Siordia, 60

music
  corrido, 52–54
  mariachi, 52–54

Nassau, Eli, 60–61

National Survey of Health and Nutrition (ENSN), 56, 57, 59, 60, 61

opinion polls. *See* surveys

Peña Nieto, Enrique, 60

Pew Research Center, 11, 55

Phypers, Jim, 15

Phypers, Mindy, 15

polls. *See* surveys

population, **7**, 11
  age of, 11–12
  indigenous, 17
  percentage of
    by ethnicity, 11
    under poverty level, 17
    by religion, 58
    in urban areas, 13

poverty, 17

Prosper program, 18

quinceañera celebration, 62–64, **63**

Ramirez, Jesús, 47

religion
   by denomination, **7**, 11, 58
   See also Catholic Church

rural life/villages, 14–16, **15**
   schools in, 32

Saylor, Stephen, 64

schools, 16
   percentage of teens attending public *vs.* private, 32
   conditions in, 12, 31–32
   See also education

Shah, Mitali, 39

Sierra, Bianca, 47–48

smartphones, prevalence of ownership of, 44

soccer, 47–48, **49**

social media, 44

sports
   professional wrestling, 48–50
   rodeo, 50–52
   soccer, 47–48

surveys
   on belief in the Virgin of Guadalupe, 61
   of Catholic Mexicans, on acceptance of church teachings, 55
   of gay teens, on respect for their rights, 60
   of teens
      on abortion, 59
      on birth control, 56
      on pregnancy, 57
   on use of contraceptives among youth, 56

teen pregnancy, 56–57

topography, 9

unemployment rates, 12

United Nations Population Fund (UNFPA), 56, 57

urban areas, homes in, **24**

urban life, 13–14

Uribe, Mónica Ortiz, 36–37

vendors, 26, **29**, 39–40

villages. *See* rural life/villages

Virgin of Guadalupe, 61

voting age, 16

water, access to, 27

Winfree, Laura, 35, 36
World Bank, 16

young people
  challenges facing, 11–13
  dating by, 44–47
  friendships among, 43–44

homeless, 14
household responsibilities of,
  26–28
prevalence of contraceptive
  use by, 56
use of social media by, 44
in workforce, 16, 37–38

PICTURE CREDITS

Barbara Sheen is the author of ninety-five nonfiction books for young people. She lives in New Mexico with her family. In her spare time she likes to swim, garden, cook, and walk.